My Family

Rosemary Dickerson

M·G·P
MARY GLASGOW PUBLICATIONS

What is a Family

A family is a group of people who are related to each other. Some families are small, some are large. All families are different. We are all part of a family even if all the members of the family do not live together.

The simplest family group is made up of one parent and one child. Many children grow up in this type of family. Perhaps the parents do not live together or one of the parents may have died. The parents might be divorced. Perhaps the child lives with her father. If he marries again his new wife will be the child's stepmother. If the child lives with her mother and the mother marries again, her new husband will be the child's stepfather. If the new stepfather or stepmother has children they will become the child's stepbrothers and stepsisters.

Often children cannot live with their real parents so they go to live with another family. The new family is called their foster family. Sometimes children are adopted and become part of a completely new family.

Your family at home is part of a much bigger family. Your parents, your brothers and sisters are your closest relatives. Then come your grandparents. They are your mother's and father's parents. Your parents' sisters and brothers are your aunts and uncles. They are close relatives too. When they marry, their husbands and wives also become your uncles and aunts. Their children will be your cousins. You are the nephews or nieces of your uncles and aunts.

Families are always changing. When people marry they bring many more people into the family. If you marry, your husband's or wife's parents become your mother-in-law and your father-in-law.

In this book you will meet children who are growing up in many different kinds of families. They have written about their families and what makes them special.

Me, My Dad and Chippy

My name is Philip. I live with my dad and my pet budgerigar, Chippingtonchipplechopples or Chippy or Chipchops for short.

I cannot remember a time when my mum was living with us because I was only two when she left. My sister Katy used to live with us but she got married and went to live in Blayton. When Katy lived with us Dad used to say "Katy do stop your chatterboxing, just for a sec, love." Now it's quiet with just Dad and me.

One day, soon after Katy got married, Dad said, "Come on, son, we could do with a pick-me-up." So we counted our pocket money and went down town to the pet shop. Inside the shop there were some budgerigars tweetering to each other. There was a blue one, a green one and a yellow one and a white one.

"Which do you fancy?" asked Dad.

We chose Chippy. She was creamy white with eyes like little black shiny berries. She put her head on one side and gave us a cheeky look. So we called her Cheeky Chippy Chipchops. That's another of her names. Dad and I make paper aeroplanes for her when she's flying about the room. She lands on them in mid-air and makes them crash into the carpet. I'm never lonely with Chippy. She chatters non-stop just like Katy used to.

At the moment my friend, Nick, is looking after Chippy because Dad and I had to move out of our flat. We had to store all our things in Nick's garage. We are in River House now. It is a large house for families who are waiting to move into a home of their own.

Sometimes Dad and I watch television in the lounge but it is very difficult because everyone else wants to talk.

I hope we will get a house soon. Our room is very cosy but it is a bit cramped. Dad has a bed. I sleep on a mattress. We put the mattress under the bed during the day. That makes more room. I don't mind what sort of house we have, but I do want to stay at my school and be near my friends Nick and Dave and keep Chippy Chipchops of course.

My dad doesn't have a job now. I like that because he is always there when I get home from school. He cooks me something nice for tea every day. Dad and I have a quiet life. We love reading and have lots of books. We have two favourite places. One is down by the river where we feed the ducks.

The other is the old railway track where we go for long walks. It is very peaceful there. Sometimes we see squirrels or birds if we're lucky. We always see something interesting. Dad is very patient and he knows a lot. He explains about things we see. Then when we get home we look for more information in some books.

Dad and I like our life but I hope we can find a house soon. Then we can unpack our things and have Chippingtonchipplechopples back.

My World Family

My family are not all in one place. They are spread all over the world. My family comes from Nigeria in Africa, but I come from London. One aunt and uncle live in America with my cousins. I was going to live with them once but I changed my mind. I like living in England where my friends are.

My parents are very busy people. My dad is an engineer in Nigeria. He works very hard and has to travel about a lot because Nigeria is a very big country. My mum lives and works in London. When I was a year old my mum brought me to my foster home where I am now.

I have lived with my big foster family for a long time and I like it that way. There are eight children in my family, including my two big sisters, so I am never lonely. Judy and Wendy have both left school and go to work.

I come next. My name is Dami and I am nine years old. Then there's Legala who is six. He has a sister Fongjang who is two. They come from a country called the Cameroons which is also in Africa.

Then there is another little family living with us. They are Andrew (five), Patrick (three) and Tina who is the baby and only one year old. It is not always fun being in the middle. Sometimes my big sisters boss me about. I don't like that but I do like it when they take me shopping on Saturdays. That makes me feel a bit more grown up than the others.

Sometimes I have to look after the younger ones. I don't mind that too much unless I want to go off and play with a friend.

I love helping Mum and Dad get Tina and Fongjang ready for bed. I like brushing their hair. Sometimes I wish someone would brush my hair.

Saturday mornings are very noisy. We are all at home. Sometimes I escape because Dad asks me to go to the post office for him. That way I can earn some pocket money. Lunch is usually hot dogs or fish and chips. We have two sittings because there isn't room at the table for all of us. The best thing about Saturday is when I'm allowed to stay up for a whole hour later than Legala.

This year I had a very big surprise. I went with my mother to Nigeria to see my family. I was very excited. The flight took about 19 hours.

I stayed with my gran near Lagos. Getting water is very difficult for her. She has no taps. The water comes from a well and it has to be boiled to clean it. Then you can have a bath. Some water comes from a tank but you have to pay for it.

My mum bought a bottle of mineral water to drink. It cost five pounds! Later I stayed with my cousins. They live in a big house. It did have taps and a video. I was very sad that I did not see my dad while I was in Nigeria. He had gone on a business trip. Instead I sent him a letter and told him all my news.

I am working hard at school because I want a good job when I grow up. Then I'll be able to visit my relations and see my dad. But I'll always come back to England because that's my home.

A Peaceful Family

My name is Christian. I live with my mum Cari, my dad Brian and my sister Amber. We live in a house stuck out in the middle of the fields. We chose our house because we like being together and we like our privacy.

Because Mum and Dad aren't married my sister and I have two surnames joined together. One is my mum's and the other is my dad's. Our name shows we belong to both of them.

My sister is only five but she is very tall. When she stands next to me she comes up to my shoulder and I am almost ten. She is called Amber because she has light ginger hair like mine.

Mum is half German but she was born in England. She has been married twice and divorced. Her first husband was my real dad but I never see him. Brian is the dad I have got now. I think of Brian as my real dad because he is the one who takes care of me.

Dad does lots of things with me. I often go for walks over the fields with him. He teases me a lot and Mum says he's not grown up himself. In the mornings he is always grumpy so we send him out to the garage. He likes to clean the car everyday. If we don't have a car for some reason there is a big problem. We don't know what to do with him!

My family is a quiet, peaceful family. We enjoy doing very ordinary things together. Our favourite day is Saturday. In the morning we go to the library to change our books. Then we have a coffee and buy our sweets and maybe get a video.

In the afternoon we might light a bonfire or watch a film on television. Then at night Mum and Dad have a curry. We call it "Cari's Curry"! My sister and I have fish fingers and chips. Then we all squeeze together on the sofa. We share our sweets and watch the video together. That's our Saturday and that's our family.

An Inquisitive Family

My name is Maureen. I was born in Holland. So were my two brothers, Robin and Justin. My mum is Dutch but my dad is English. So we are half Dutch and half English. I'm not sure about my little sister Gillian. She was born in France when we moved there from Holland, so I think she must be a bit English, a bit Dutch and a bit French!

I speak English at school of course, except when I have a French lesson. But at home we all speak Dutch. I think that is what makes my family special. It is our secret. Most of my friends think I'm English like them. They don't know I speak Dutch at home.

Christmas is especially nice in our family because we have two. We have our Dutch Christmas on 5 December when Santa Claus comes and gives us an orange and other presents. This year we will have to go to school on that day. It's on a Monday!

My family is very noisy. We laugh a lot and we also quarrel a lot. We are definitely not peaceful.

There's a special reason why we quarrel. It always starts in the same way. We are all very inquisitive! It gets us into a lot of trouble. One day it was snowing very hard. Some cars got stuck in the road outside our house. My brothers and my little sister rushed into my bedroom to have a look out of the window.

Mum heard us. She was in the kitchen and she didn't want to miss one bit of what was going on. She raced up the stairs, tripped at the top and fell into my bedroom. I was the only one who saw her. I laughed out loud. She got very cross at first but then we all ended up laughing.

My little sister is the most adventurous of us all. When we went on a camping holiday she kept wandering off into other people's tents.

My dad's curiosity shows in a different way. He can't stand being indoors. He loves going out on Saturdays and Sundays. So when he says, "Let's go for a drive," everybody has to go with him. We can't wait. The rest of us are just as inquisitive.

My favourite time is in the evening when my brothers and little sister have gone to bed. I have a little time on my own with Mummy and Daddy. Sometimes we play a game or they read me a story or we just chat. Then Mum tucks me up in bed. She kisses me and whispers "Welterusten" (rest well). I say "Welterusten" back. Then I go to sleep.

A Famous Family

My family is the most active, healthy family I know. My family is not allowed to lie in on Sunday morning. We are all up by seven o'clock and by eight o'clock we are down at the swimming baths doing our training.

My dad is in the Master Class. He trains on Wednesday as well. My sister, Delyth, is good at netball and swimming. My mum keeps fit everyday. She is a PE teacher.

There is one thing about our family that never changes. That is our summer holiday. Every year we have to go to the Lake District. Mum and Dad take us there to get plenty of fresh air and exercise. Everyday we climb and walk over all the Lake District. My body aches all over. Sometimes I wish I belonged to an ordinary, lazy family that likes sitting on the beach all day.

Rugby is our other interest. Our cousin, Stephen, plays for the Wasps in London. We go all over the country watching him play rugby. This year we were all very proud because Stephen was picked as reserve for England's scrum half against Australia.

ENGLAND
White Jerseys, White Shorts

Referee:
D. J. Bishop (New Zealand)
Touch Judges:
R. J. Megson (S.R.U.)
J. M. Fleming (S.R.U.)

AUSTRALIA
Gold Jerseys, Green Shorts

England		Position	Australia	
15.	J. M. WEBB, Bristol	FULL BACK	15.	A. J. LEEDS, Paramatta, Sydney
		THREE QUARTERS		
14.	† A. T. HARRIMAN, Harlequins	RIGHT WING	14.	J. C. GRANT, Orange City, N.S.W.
13.	W. D. C. CARLING (captain), Harlequins	CENTRE	13.	† B. GIRVAN, Norths, Canberra
12.	S. J. HALLIDAY, Bath	CENTRE	12.	M. T. COOK, University, Brisbane
11.	R. UNDERWOOD, RAF & Leicester	LEFT WING	11.	D. I. CAMPESE, Randwick
		HALF BACKS		
10.	C. R. ANDREW, Wasps	STAND-OFF	10.	M. P. LYNAGH, University, Brisbane
9.	† C. D. MORRIS, Liverpool St. Helens	SCRUM-HALF	9.	N. C. FARR-JONES (captain), Sydney University
		FORWARDS		
1.	P. A. G. RENDALL, Wasps	PROP	1.	M. N. HARTILL, Gordon, Sydney
2.	B. C. MOORE, Nottingham	HOOKER	2.	T. A. LAWTON, Souths, Brisbane
3.	J. A. PROBYN, Wasps	PROP	3.	A. J. McINTYRE, University, Brisbane
4.	W. A. DOOLEY, Preston Grasshoppers	LOCK	4.	S. A. G. CUTLER, Gordon, Sydney
5.	† P. J. ACKFORD, Harlequins	LOCK	5.	W. A. CAMPBELL, Wests, Brisbane
6.	R. A. ROBINSON, Bath	FLANKER	6.	J. S. MILLER, University, Brisbane
7.	D. W. EGERTON, Bath	FLANKER	7.	J. M. GARDNER, Wests, Brisbane
8.	D. RICHARDS, Leicester	No. 8	8.	S. N. TUYNMAN, Eastwood, Sydney

† New cap

Replacements: 16. J.R.D. Buckton (Saracens) 17. A.L. Thompson (Harlequins) 18. S.M. Bates (Wasps) 19. G.J. Chilcott (Bath) 20. K. Dunn (Gloucester) 21. G.W. Rees (Nottingham)

Replacements: 16. B. T. Burke (Randwick) 17. L. F. Walker (Randwick) 18. A. S. Niuqila (Randwick) 19. M. I. McBain (Brothers, Brisbane) 20. R. Lawton (Souths, Brisbane) 21. T. B. Gavin (Eastern Suburbs, Sydney)

KICK-OFF 2.30 p.m.

The Rugby Football Union gratefully acknowledge the support of Save & Prosper

SAVE & PROSPER THE INVESTMENT HOUSE

24

25

My family all went to Twickenham to see the match. Morris was the name of England's scrum half. On the way there I said "I hope Morris gets injured, so Stephen can play," But Delyth said "Don't be horrible, Emily." I knew Delyth was right but I couldn't help wanting Stephen to play. Morris scored a try and he did get injured. I thought it was my fault! Mum, Dad and I hoped he would get taken off but he wasn't.

After the match we went to the Rose Room where all the players go after a special game. My cousin came in. He gave Delyth and me a kiss. Then he presented us with a little rugby ball each. They were signed with his name.

Then I felt pleased that we were a sporty family and very lucky that I had such a famous cousin.